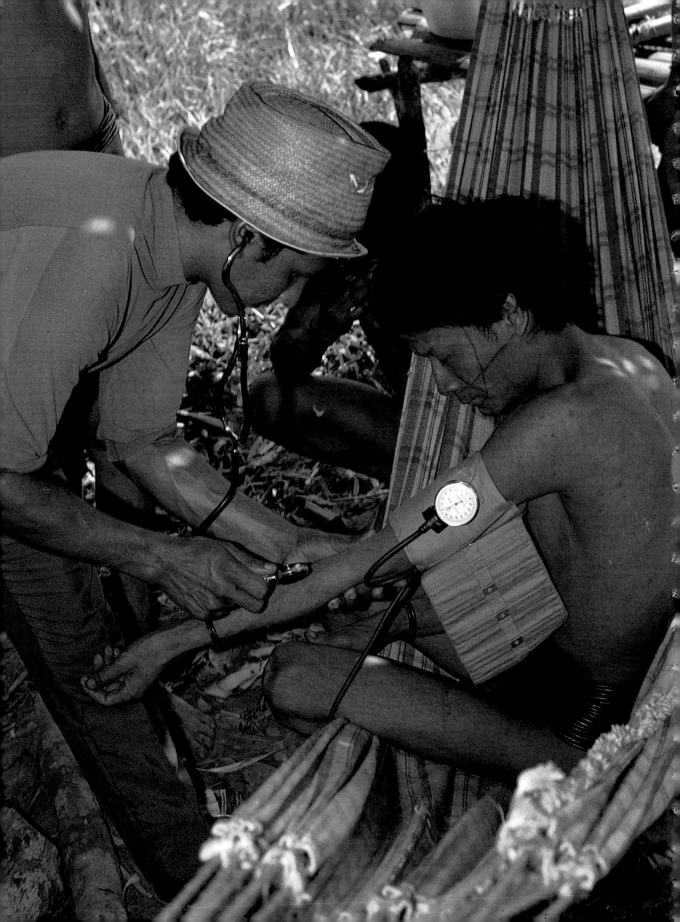

WORLD HEALTH

Janie Hampton

4230108

ROURKE ENTERPRISES INC.
Vero Beach, Florida 32964

World Issues

Endangered Wildlife
Food or Famine?
Nuclear Weapons
Population Growth
Terrorism
The Arms Trade
The Energy Crisis
The Environment
The International Drug Trade
World Health

Cover: A mother in Lesotho administering an Oral Rehydration Drink.
Frontispiece: Vaccination of a member of the Surui tribe in the Brazilian Amazon.

Text © 1988 Rourke Enterprises Inc.
PO Box 3328, Vero Beach, Florida 32964

Printed in Italy.

Library of Congress Cataloging in Publication Data
Hampton, Janie, 1949 –
    World Health/Janie Hampton.
        p.   cm. — (World issues)
        Bibliography: p.
        Includes index.
        ISBN 0–86592–281–0
        1. World health — Juvenile literature. I. Title.   II. Series:
    World issues (Vero Beach, Fla.)
    RA441.H36 1988
362.1—dc19   87–38309
                                                                CIP
                                                                AC

Contents

1
A divided world

"Health is complete physical, mental and social well-being and not merely the absence of disease."

World Health Organization (WHO) definition

Being healthy means being fit for daily life, having reserves of strength, and freedom from pain or disease. Most people would agree that everyone in the world has a right to good health, but many of the world's people do not get a chance to enjoy it.

North and South

In those parts of the world where food is scarce and living conditions are poor, it is easy for illness to attack people. Rich countries, too, have health problems. There, illness is often caused by an affluent lifestyle.

It is convenient, if not entirely accurate, to refer to these two different worlds, the rich and the poor, as the North and the South. If you look at the diagram on this page, you will see that most of the world's wealth is possessed by the industrialized countries of North America and Europe, in the northern part of the world. The poorer countries lie mostly in the southern area. Throughout this book we shall use the shorthand terms "North" and "South" to refer to this division between the rich and poor areas of the world.

This map shows how wealth is concentrated largely in the northern countries.

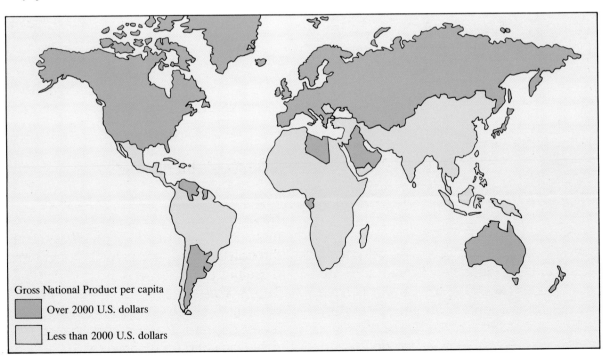

Gross National Product per capita

Over 2000 U.S. dollars

Less than 2000 U.S. dollars

Although there is much ill health in the North, conditions in the poor South are far worse. For every $100 spent on health care on a person in the North, less than $2 is spent in the South. The South has 75 percent of the world's people, but only 30 percent of the world's food grains, 15 percent of the world's energy and 6 percent of the world's health spending. Most people in the South have too little food, fuel, education, transportation and water. When there are world shortages, we in the North still have enough, but those in the South suffer. They have low incomes and do not benefit from science and technology, as we do.

A Bangladeshi slum. Poor living conditions in the South are the main reason why there is more ill health there than in the North.

Health care for the world

The state of health care in the South can be understood by looking at its development in the North. Every country goes through three periods of health care. First, there must be improved living conditions. This includes better diet, clean water and efficient sanitation. These basic improvements depend on the decisions made by politicians and on technology.

9

The next stage, once public health standards have been improved, is for individual care by doctors to be introduced. They can prevent and treat disease using immunization, medicines and operations in hospitals.

The third stage is when improvements in individual lifestyle and in the environment are introduced by governments and industry. In the United States, over 6,000 people die each week from smoking-related diseases. Nearly 600 people die each week from gunshot wounds. To reduce these figures, the U.S. government would have to make major decisions about smoking and the possession of firearms.

In the North, we have achieved the first and second stages and are now entering stage three. In the South, the first and second stages are happening together, so child deaths are falling and population is increasing dramatically.

It is difficult to measure the health of a population, but one can measure the number of deaths, the causes of death and the age when it occurs. This gives us an idea of the health of the country. Life expectancy (the average age people live to) is over 70 years in the North, but under 50 years in some parts of the South. For every 1,000 babies born in Zambia, 135 will die in their first year. In the U.S., that figure is 10.5 per 1,000. In Japan, it is even lower: 7 per 1,000. In Britian, the figure is 13 per 1,000.

In the North, cancer kills one in five people. Some of this cancer is caused by smoking, food additives, pollution and radiation. One in three people will die from heart disease, caused by bad diet, lack of exercise, stress and smoking. The major causes of death in the South are not, as you might expect, tropical diseases such as malaria and cholera, but the same

A pie-chart showing the different health problems that predominate in the North and South.

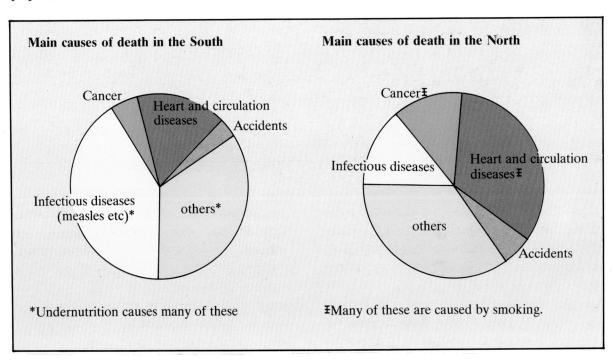

Main causes of death in the South

Cancer

Heart and circulation diseases

Accidents

Infectious diseases (measles etc)*

others*

*Undernutrition causes many of these

Main causes of death in the North

Cancer‡

Heart and circulation diseases‡

Infectious diseases

others

Accidents

‡Many of these are caused by smoking.

This cartoon, published in 1852, shows the dreadful squalor of a London slum. Many of the infectious diseases that are still prevalent in the South would have been common there.

curable and preventable diseases that killed most people in Europe until about 150 years ago: tuberculosis (TB), measles, pneumonia and diarrhea. These are caused by poverty and undernutrition, rather than lack of doctors. Most of the disability that affects people in the South could be prevented by better nutrition, immunization against disease and safer living and working conditions.

Population

In the North, families tend to have fewer children, and very few of these babies die in infancy. Most people in the more affluent countries can expect to live until retirement and beyond. The situation in the poor countries, however, is quite different. In the South, families have more babies, and many of these babies die. Parents will choose to have fewer babies only when they know the children have a good chance of survival. This is because children are the only resource, or wealth, that poor parents have, especially in rural areas. The children of poor farmers are needed to help on the land, look after the smaller children and support their parents in old age. By the time a boy is fifteen years old, he has refunded his parents' investment in his food and clothes. By contrast, an American child costs his or her parents an average of $100,000 over eighteen years.

Once a country's infant mortality rate drops, the birthrate drops one generation

By the time they are six years old, many children in the South are earning their living on the land or in factories.

later, because parents no longer need to have many babies to ensure that some survive. Most women do not want to have very large families. Once they are in control of their own lives, free from illiteracy and oppression, they will choose to limit the number of their children.

Population growth, however, is still a

This young girl cannot go to school because she is responsible for looking after her younger brothers and sisters.

problem. At the present rate of increase, one new teacher is needed in the South every minute. In Austria (a wealthy northern country) there is one elementary

13

school teacher for every 23 school-age children, but in Bangladesh there is only one for every 77 children. Secondary schools have even fewer teachers. In 1970 those children of elementary school age who were *not* attending school could encircle the world three times. By 1985 they could encircle the world four times. These are problems that must be tackled if world health is to improve.

A classroom in Bangladesh. Schools in the South are often overcrowded, have no furniture and very few books.

2
Child health

"The most important goal is to protect the development of the next generation of children – both to defend the child's right to life and to invest in the progress of the poor world. For there is a fundamental connection between the physical and mental development of children and the social and economic development of their nations."

State of the World's Children Report,
UNICEF, 1986

In the North, the infant mortality and birth-rates have already fallen and there are now fewer children than adults. In parts of the South, however, almost half of the population is under fifteen years old, because the birthrate is still high and more children are surviving. Even so, every year in the South, 12 to 18 *million* children under the age of five die. Five million of them die from dehydration caused by common diarrhea; 3 million die from pneumonia; 2 million die from measles (and many more are blinded by it); 1.5 million die from whooping cough. Half of the children in the South die before they are fifteen. Most of these deaths could be prevented by cheap and simple technologies.

Children are the group most vulnerable to infectious and parasitic diseases.

Comparing North with South

One way we can compare the health of children in different parts of the world is to take two groups and look at them in detail. For example, we could compare the average figures for children in a developed country in the North with those for a similar age group in Central Africa. If we took ten children in their second year of life in the North, we would find (on average) that they had had among them:

10 colds
1 pneumonia
2 measles
2 diarrhea
1 skin infection
0 malaria
1 born weighing less than 4½ lb (2 kg), perhaps because the mother smoked cigarettes during pregancy.

Approximately $350 per year is spent on health care for each child in the North.

If we then look at ten children in their second year of life in Central Africa, we find that, on average, they will have had among them:

17 colds
4 pneumonia
4 measles
20 diarrhea
16 skin infections
26 malaria
2 born underweight because their mothers were malnourished.

An average of $5 a year is spent on the health care of each child in the South.

Each of these illnesses will be more dangerous than they would be in the North, because the child will have less food to eat and may not have recovered from the last illness. Only one of these ten

children will ever see a health worker. Later they will have only two years at school, on average.

Food

About two-thirds of children under five years old in the South are undernourished. Most do not look as bad as children in the magazine ads for Save the Children, but they are weak and thin for their age. Few will ever have protein-rich foods such as meat, fish, and eggs, but these foods are not essential for growth and good health. More important are energy-giving, high-calorie foods such as cooking oil, margarine and peanut butter. Staple foods like plantain bananas, corn, potatoes and cassava contain too much water and not enough calories. Small children cannot eat enough of these bulky foods to make them grow well.

Undernourished children have less resistance to disease, so they fall ill more

Premature or underweight babies in the North receive intensive medical care. This child would probably have died if she had been born in the South.

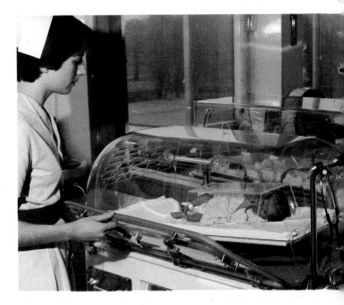

often and take longer to recover – if they survive. They do not grow so tall and strong, and can be physically damaged in various ways. For example, shortage of Vitamin A (which is found in orange-colored fruit and vegetables and in green leafy vegetables) is a worldwide problem. Every year 14,000 children in India alone are permanently blinded by a lack of sufficient Vitamin A.

One of the major problems is that shortage of the correct food produces a vicious circle of deprivation and suffering. Small undernourished mothers produce small weak babies. Small undernourished fathers cannot find work, so their families suffer. The average weight of women in the United States is 128 pounds (58 kg); in Central America it is 110 pounds (50 kg) and in India it is only 99 pounds (45 kg). Enough food to feed the whole world is the most important health priority.

Diarrhea

Diarrhea is the world's major killer, killing 10,000 to 20,000 children *every day*. The main causes of diarrhea are undernourishment, dirty water, poor hygiene, bottle feeding, lack of latrines (toilets), infestation by worms and eating rotten foods. Children in the poorer countries get diarrhea on average ten times a year, which makes them even more undernourished because they are unable to absorb nutrients from their food. Diarrhea kills by dehydration – loss of water and salts from the body. The body is made of 60 percent water and cannot function without it. Just as a plant wilts and dies without water, so does a human body.

Bottle feeding is one of the major causes of diarrhea and malnutrition in the developing countries.

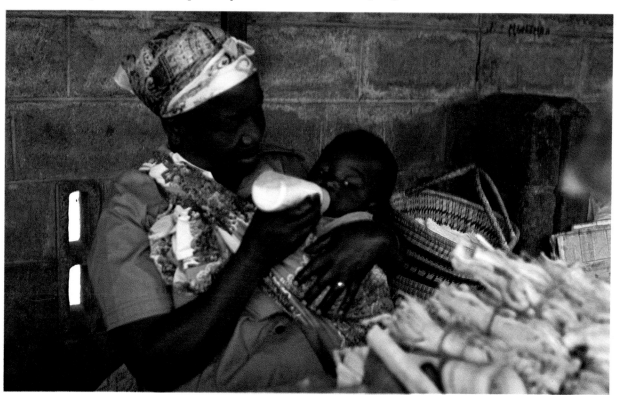

Dehydration can be prevented and cured in the home with Oral Rehydration Drink, which is a simple mixture of water, sugar and salt. The sugar helps the body absorb the salt. Diarrhea is the body's way of flushing out germs. Medicines do not help diarrhea, or dehydration, because they hold the germs inside the body. Giving water and salt by injection is expensive and not as safe as by mouth. The Oral Rehydration Drink is effective, easy to make and easily administered. Parents and children all over the world are now being taught how to make it. Already at least 200,000 lives a year are being saved by this simple method.

Measles were controlled in the U.S. with vaccinations. Before 1963, annual cases averaged 400,000 to 800,000. Now just 1,500 to 3,000 cases occur each year.

> Never in the history of medicine has so much been done for so many with so simple a technology and so little expenditure.
> *Dr. Mamdouh Gabr, Minister of Health for Egypt, speaking of the Oral Rehydration Drink program*

Childhood diseases

The six major childhood diseases are measles, whooping cough, polio, tuberculosis (TB), diphtheria and tetanus. Nowadays these are rare in North America and Europe, but they killed or disabled many children until quite recent times. All these diseases can be prevented by immunization and good nutrition. Measles is the deadliest of these diseases, causing diarrhea, pneumonia or blindness and

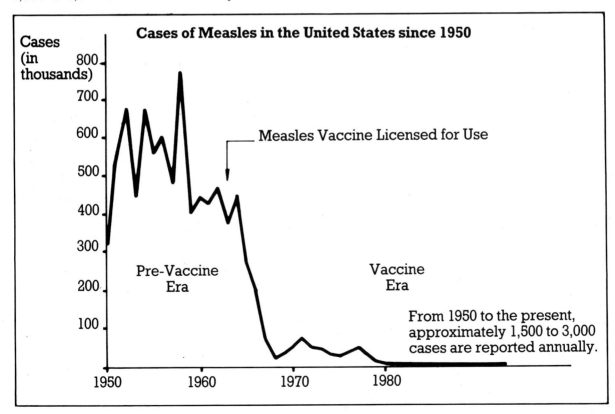

Cases of Measles in the United States since 1950

Cases (in thousands)

Measles Vaccine Licensed for Use

Pre-Vaccine Era

Vaccine Era

From 1950 to the present, approximately 1,500 to 3,000 cases are reported annually.

killing 2.5 million children every year.

Now that these child-killing illnesses are largely controlled in the North, accidents are the most common cause of death among children there. Most of these accidents could be prevented. In the United States, over 20 children die accidentally

An Indian mother with her young son, who has been blinded by measles.

each day. Although most of these deaths are due to car accidents, many children also drown or die in fires.

How to make an Oral Rehydration Drink
1. Wash out a one-pint milk bottle.
2. Fill the bottle with clean water.
3. Mix in half a level teaspoon of salt.
4. *Taste* the drink. If it is more salty than tears, throw it away and start again.
5. Mix in five teaspoons of sugar, or honey.
6. If possible, mix in the juice of an orange or half a mashed banana. These contain potassium, an important mineral.

Experiment with different amounts of salt and sugar. The drink should never taste more salty than tears. If you put in too much sugar, the diarrhea may get worse; if you use too much salt, dehydration increases. In many countries measured packages of sugar and salt are given to parents to be mixed with water. In other countries mothers are taught how to mix the drink correctly by using local standard measures such as matchboxes and bottle tops.

A woman in Somalia being instructed in Oral Rehydration. Ensuring that all mothers know about this therapy should be one of our top health priorities.

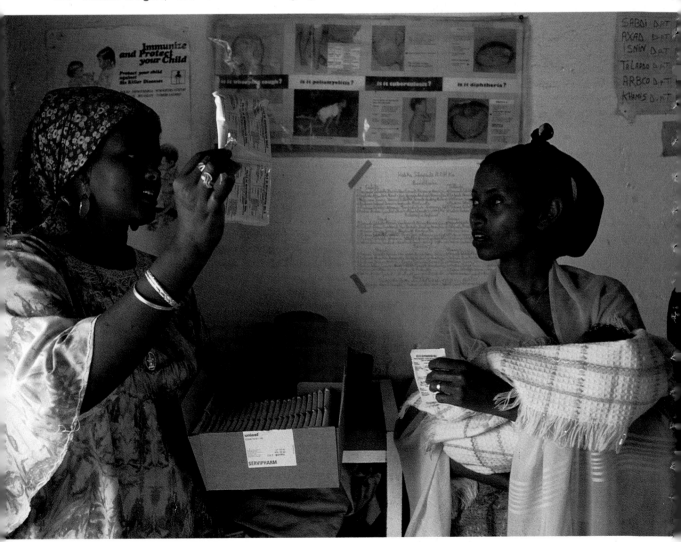

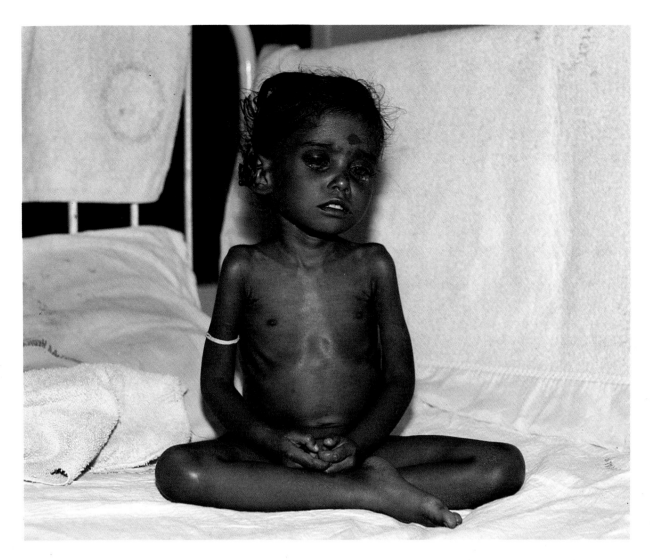

Although this child is now receiving food and medicine, malnutrition has already damaged her physical and mental development.

Present knowledge holds out the opportunity to halve the rate of child malnutrition and child death at a relatively low cost and in a relatively short time.
State of the World's Children report, UNICEF, 1986

We are guilty of many errors and many faults, but our worst crime is abandoning the children, neglecting the fountain of life.
Many things can wait.
The Child cannot.
Right now is the time her bones are being formed, her blood is being made and her senses are being developed.
To her we cannot answer "Tomorrow."
Her name is "Today."

Gabriela Mistral, Nobel Prize-winning poet from Chile

21

3 Curing illness

Curative health care means treating those people already suffering from diseases and accidental injury. This kind of health care affects the health of the individual, not the health of the community as a whole. Curative health care is also expensive. It costs a great deal to train doctors, to buy medicines, buildings and equipment and to maintain them. Such high-technology medicine as a heart transplant does not prolong many lives, but it makes news and gives prestige to governments and specialist doctors. Five heart transplants cost the same as 4,000 hip replacement operations, which could make old people mobile and free from pain. Satyajit Ray, a popular Indian film maker, was sent by his government to the United States for a heart operation that cost 700,000 rupees – the same as the total spending on 100,000 people in some Indian states.

Modern surgery often has dramatic results, but it uses a huge amount of medical resources that might have helped many more people.

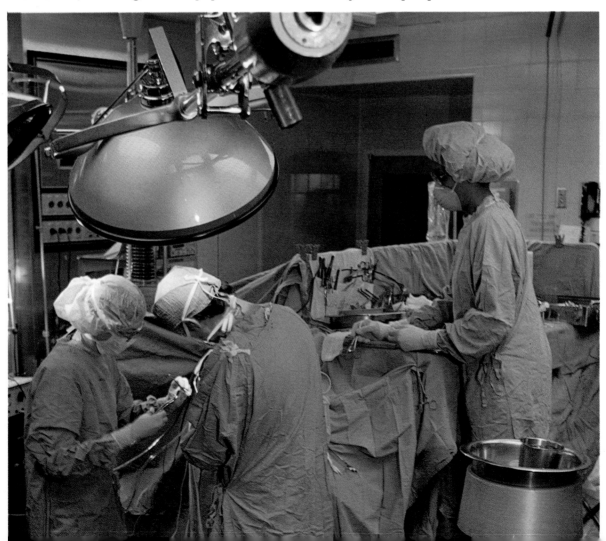

Doctors and hospitals do not necessarily make people healthy. Often they are treating diseases that could have been prevented in the first place. Much money is spent treating lung cancer, heart disease and high blood pressure. These conditions could usually be prevented if we change our living habits.

Signing the check for a heart care unit may be signing the death certificate for thousands of children whose lives could have been saved if the money were used differently.

British health expert, 1986

A street vendor in Zaïre selling antibiotics, contraceptive pills and other potentially dangerous drugs as single tablets. Most of them are useless unless a full course is taken and many are out-of-date.

Medicines

Although medicines are important in treating diseases, they have a much smaller role to play in keeping us healthy. The invention of antibiotics and immunization has prevented the deaths of many children, but not as many as have been saved by being given more food, clean water and better living conditions.

Drugs and medicines are used too much everywhere in the world. Patients now expect them, and doctors give them. In many countries there are few restrictions on medicines, and so anyone can buy them in markets or on street corners. They are often out of date or dangerous, but the seller does not understand this. Pharmaceutical companies make large profits by selling untested or banned medicines in the South. In the North, medicines may not be sold without careful tests and research. Even so, people have died or been disabled after being given dangerous medicines.

Traditional healers

In the South, most health care and treatment is given not by hospital-trained doctors but by traditional healers. They may not be highly trained at medical schools but they often understand more about local conditions and diseases than specialist doctors or nurses. Many governments have recognized the value of traditional health workers and are now cooperating with them rather than trying to replace them. In Zimbabwe and Somalia, for example, traditional midwives work with the local maternity hospitals, where they learn about hygiene. They deliver most babies in the mothers' homes, but take them to hospital if there are any problems. The mothers have safer home births than they used to have, as well as special treatment if it is needed, at a much lower cost. Traditional healers and trained nurses in Swaziland are now working together successfully, sharing ideas and knowledge about preventing and treating disease.

Community health workers

Community health workers can save more lives than specialist doctors. They have the special advantage of being chosen by their community and trained in it, so they remain part of it. They share their knowledge with those most in need, not just those who can afford to pay the most. For the cost of one doctor there can be hundreds of community health workers. There are four countries in Africa with no medical schools at all, but which have excellent child health services.

Community health centers and small clinics are closer to the patients, so they can treat patients earlier. Where transportation is scarce or expensive, many sick people cannot afford to go to a hospital.

Doctors trained in large hospitals often think about the money they will earn when they are specialist consultants, especially if they have large medical school bills to pay off. Doctors are trained to diagnose rare

This girl was born crippled because her mother took a drug called thalidomide during pregrancy.

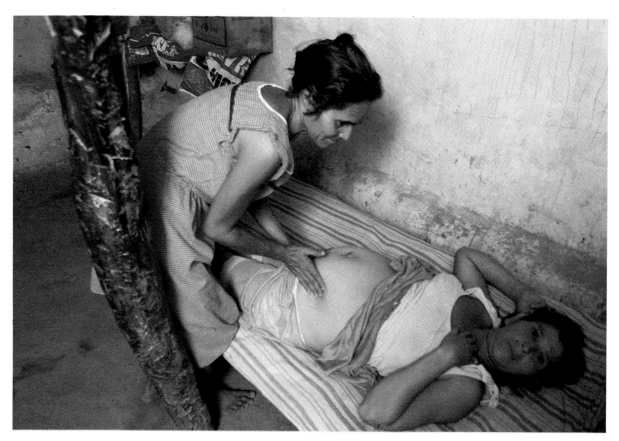

diseases, and their specialized skills are not needed to treat common illnesses. Community health workers learn how to prevent disease and promote good health. But everyone who is sick deserves medical treatment, even if the illness could have been prevented. Curative and preventive medicine must balance one another.

Health for All, not Health For a Few

In the South, 85 percent of health spending goes on curative care for 10 percent of the people. The remaining money is spread out over 90 percent of the people and used for preventive primary health care. For example, in Kenya, 60 percent of doctors work in Nairobi, the capital city, but 75 percent of the people live outside the capital in rural areas.

A community midwife in Honduras. Local midwives have a vital role to play in pre- and post-natal care as well as during birth.

Below *Community health workers do not need expensive facilities. They advise people about preventive care and simple ailments in their own villages.*

4 Preventing illness

Preventive health care does not depend on doctors, hospitals and medicines, but on education about ways of staying healthy so that we do not need these things. Preventive health care is cheap. It is difficult to introduce but has a great effect on the improvement of health in the whole community. It is easy to cure someone of malaria with medicines, or vaccinate them against smallpox, but persuading people to give up smoking, or to eat different food, or to use a latrine, is much more difficult.

In the North, the things that promote health and prevent disease are taken for granted. Health for all cannot be achieved until living conditions are improved everywhere in the world.

Sewage from these shanties in Brazil is poured straight into the lake whose water is then used for washing and drinking.

Clean water and sanitation

Only 29 percent of people in countries like Malawi and Burma have access to clean water. Lack of safe water and sanitation is the cause of 80 percent of the world's diseases. In many areas, people have to walk long distances every day to collect water, so they use as little water

Collecting water in Mexico. Piped water in the home is a luxury enjoyed by very few people in the world.

as possible. Having a good supply of clean water prevents diarrhea, skin infections and many water-borne diseases such as typhoid and cholera. Clean water can be provided by village wells or pumps.

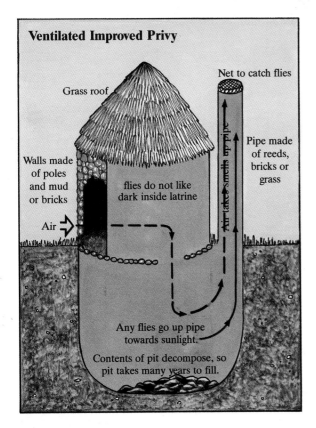

Ventilated Improved Privy

Grass roof

Net to catch flies

Pipe made of reeds, bricks or grass

Walls made of poles and mud or bricks

flies do not like dark inside latrine

Air takes smells up pipe

Air

Any flies go up pipe towards sunlight.

Contents of pit decompose, so pit takes many years to fill.

This picture shows the features of a Ventilated Improved Privy, which are important in preventing the spread of disease.

Flushing toilets are expensive and use too much water for countries where there is little rain. One solution is the Ventilated Improved Privy (VIP), an outhouse that uses available materials and is cheap to build. The VIP was developed in Zimbabwe, Africa, and many schools, clinics and homes there now have them.

GOBI

UNICEF has proposed four health priorities for children, known by the first letters of each: GOBI.

Growth checking. If children are weighed every month, then their growth can be recorded on a special chart and monitored easily. The health workers can give the mother advice if the child is not growing well, which may be due to illness or lack of food. In Indonesia 2.5 million children are weighed at monthly women's meetings. The mothers keep the growth cards so that wherever they go they have a record of the child's growth, immunizations and illnesses.

Oral rehydration – see page 18. Teaching people how to make an Oral Rehydration Drink combats the world's greatest killer: diarrhea.

Breastfeeding is best. Breast milk contains no germs. It contains antibodies and vitamins to fight off disease. It is always available. It is made especially for human babies. It prevents pregnancy, and it is free! Breastfeeding is especially important in poor areas without clean water supplies. Breastfeeding a child for two years is not a "primitive" custom – it makes stronger, healthier children. Mothers in the North are now also realizing the importance of long-term breastfeeding.

Immunization against the major childhood diseases prevents death and disability and costs about $5 a child. During 1986, about a million lives were saved by immunization – but over 3 million children died because they were not immunized. Every year, over a quarter of a million children are paralyzed for life by polio. Two drops of polio vaccine given on three occasions will stop this. By immunizing all their babies, most of the United States is now free of measles. The eradication of measles from the whole world is possible. But vaccines have to be kept cold all the time or they stop working, and parents

Checking the weight of a malnourished nine-year-old in Honduras. An adequate diet is the most important medicine.

must understand the importance of immunization.

In Brazil, the army, churches, schools and political parties all work together to immunize every small child in the country on one day every year. On three Sundays in 1985, the civil war in El Salvador, in Central America, was stopped so that two-thirds of the nation's children could be immunized. This is more effective than immunizing those few children who attend health clinics. In the North, 85 percent of children are immunized against measles. In Africa it is 35 percent, and in South and East Asia only 10 percent.

Smallpox has been eradicated thanks to a worldwide immunization program.

Breastfeeding is the best form of nutrition for all babies everywhere in the world.

But immunization will always be necessary for some diseases, such as tetanus, which cannot be completely overcome.

Birth spacing

This is another vital factor in world health care. A mother who has a baby every year has little time and energy to look after her other children. If she waits three years between each birth she has time to look after the child and to breastfeed it for at least two years. While a mother is breastfeeding she is unlikely to get pregnant again. More births are prevented by breastfeeding than by contraceptives, although contraceptives are more reliable. Making it possible to have a space of two to three years between births improves the growth, health and intelligence of children all over the world.

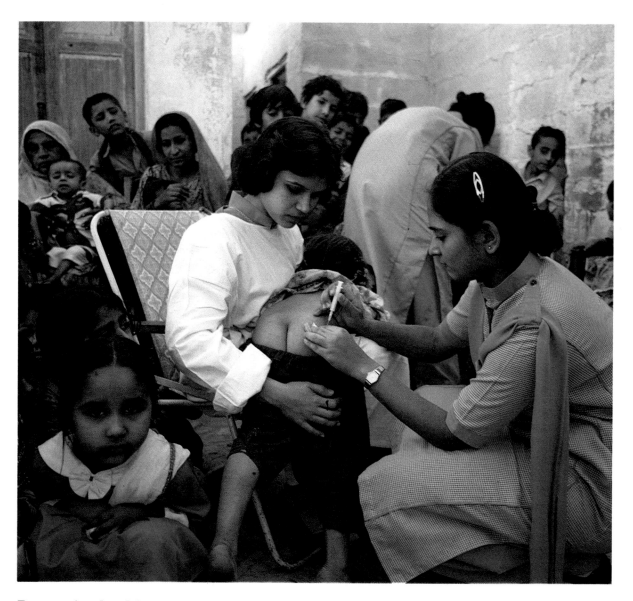

Preventive health care in the North

In the countries of the industrialized North, there has been more money to spend on preventive health care. People in the richer countries can take for granted that their sewage is efficiently removed and treated. The amount of pollution released into the air and water by industry is also monitored.

Special care is taken of babies and young children, with mothers being able

Immunization at a child health clinic in Pakistan. A major problem with immunization programs in the South is keeping vaccines cold.

to receive pre-natal care at clinics and hospitals. They are also encouraged to breastfeed their babies and to have them immunized and are helped to provide them with nutritious food.

Health education is an important part of this process. Car users are frequently

31

Antismoking poster aimed at children. If people do not smoke in their teens, then they are unlikely to begin.

warned of the hazards of drinking and driving, and campaigns and legislation to make the wearing of seat belts compulsory have been successful in making driving safer. Similarly, people are frequently reminded by the health educators about the dangers of alcohol and drug abuse, and the importance of safety in the home and at work, and the perils of smoking.

Unfortunately not everyone acts upon this advice. Alcohol is still responsible for a large number of fatal car accidents and accidents that happen at work. Antismoking campaigns have managed to ban some cigarette advertising and have had many

public places declared nonsmoking areas, but there is still a long way to go.

In the North, huge sums of money are spent each year on advertising tobacco products. Only a tiny fraction of the same amount is spent on health education. Smoking still causes over 300,000 deaths in the United States every year. The number of smokers has declined, however. But, as smoking decreases in the North, tobacco companies are concentrating their sales efforts in the South, where smoking has increased 33 percent in the last decade.

AIDS

The latest health education campaign in the North aims to alert people to the dangers of AIDS, which stands for Acquired Immune Deficiency Syndrom. People with AIDS lose their natural immunity to all diseases; an AIDS victim may die of anything from a common infection to a rare form of cancer.

AIDS was only discovered in 1979, but since then it has been spreading all over the world. No one knows why or how it started. Compared with many diseases, AIDS is still rare, but there is no known cure for it. Those who have AIDS in their blood can give it to someone else through sexual contact, infected injection needles or from blood transfusions. Countries in the North can afford to use new, sterile needles for all injections and to test blood for AIDS before transfusions, but these precautions are expensive, and the South cannot afford them. Neither can it afford such a massive health education campaign. AIDS may well become one of the world's major health problems within the next decade.

5 Health and Politics

Health for all cannot be achieved by simply building more hospitals and training more doctors. More important to the health of the population at large is the equal distribution of resources, both across the world and within countries. This can only be achieved by politicians. Politicians keep people healthy – or allow them to fall ill – by deciding how the country's wealth will be distributed among the people. Housing, roads, schools, hospitals, agriculture, armies, taxation and trade – how these are dealt with by politicians will affect that nation's health.

How politics and health are linked

In China, politicians have improved the health of the people. Within 15 years of the revolution in 1949, the child death rate fell from 200 per 1,000 to less than 20. This caused the population to increase more in 10 years than in the previous 100 years. Now couples with only one child are rewarded with large salaries and higher pensions in the hope that this will reduce population growth. Agricultural land

In general, the richer a country, the longer the life expectancy of its people. China deviates from the pattern because of its fair distribution of resources and effective primary health care system.

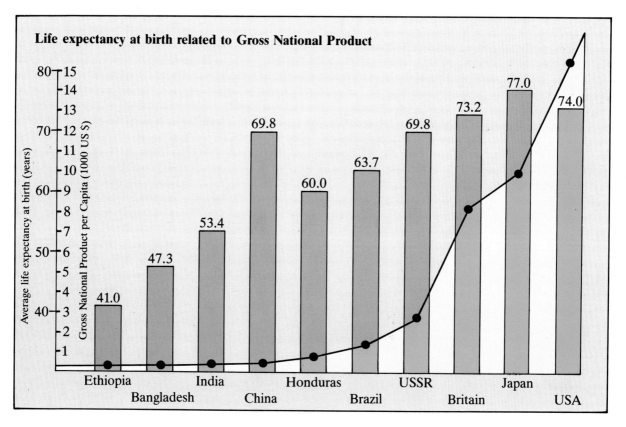

Life expectancy at birth related to Gross National Product

has been more fairly distributed in order to increase food production, reduce poverty and improve health.

In Latin America, rich landowners have the best land, which they use for cattle ranching and growing export crops. Small farmers help to improve health more than large landowners, because they grow food for home use. In Brazil, the small farmers have only 21 percent of the land, but grow 73 percent of the food.

Although the countries of the South are poor, there are some rich people in those countries. These rich people make the laws and decide how to distribute the resources. They do not want to lose their wealth, so they direct resources for their own benefit. In South Africa, 74 percent of the people are black, but they are ruled by the white minority. Blacks there receive less care than the whites; consequently, their infant mortality rate is 5 times higher than the whites' rate and they have 11 times more measles cases.

Harvesting sugar on a plantation in St. Kitts, an island in the Caribbean Sea. Much of the best land in the South is used to grow crops for export rather than food for the local people.

What can governments do to improve health?

First, in all countries, governments could spend less money on defense and more on saving lives. Most governments are more interested in armies than in health or education. They ignore statistics such as these:

$1 billion can be used to create 76,000 new jobs in the army, or 139,000 jobs in health, or 187,000 jobs in education.

100 children can be educated for the cost of training and arming one soldier.

500,000 new homes can be built for the cost of one nuclear submarine.

50,000 village pharmacies can be

Health programs are in direct competition with military projects for a country's human and financial resources.

equipped for the cost of one jet fighter.

In the North, an average of $350 per year is spent per person on health. In the South, it is under $10. In some countries it is even less, especially for the rural poor. Providing clean water, sanitation, trained workers and basic drugs would cost an extra $15 per person per year. This would amount in total to two-thirds of world spending on cigarettes or half of world spending on alcohol or one-fifth of world spending on armies.

Second, farmers could be encouraged to change their crops so that they would grow soybeans rather than keeping animals for meat, or grow wheat rather than tobacco. Food is the most important of all resources for good health. Undernutrition of children is increasing in the South, because more land is being used for nonfood crops such as tobacco, coffee, and for sugar cane for processing into gasoline. Most of these crops are exported to the North.

Much of the grain grown in the South is exported to the North, where it feeds cattle, pigs and chickens. These well-fed animals provide us with our meat-rich diet. For every three bags of grain used in the North, one is available for a population the same size in the South. People go hungry in the South, but cows in the North eat well.

This family in Kenya are using their land to grow beans, which are an excellent source of cheap protein.

They eat energy and protein concentrates that could have been used as food for people in the South.

Encouraging breastfeeding could do much to improve world health. In Papua New Guinea, for example, breastfeeding has increased and diarrhea and malnutrition have been reduced since the government banned the sale of baby bottles in stores. If well-known women such as presidents, princesses and movie stars are known to breastfeed their babies, other mothers will copy them.

Cattle being fed grain-based concentrates. Eating meat and dairy products is a very wasteful way of consuming protein.

If more political power is given to the people, they can decide for themselves how they want resources to be distributed. In the South of the world, most health care expenditure occurs in cities, where the minority of the people live.

Even in the U.S., rich people receive better health care than poor people. Those who can afford to buy health insurance are much more likely to seek medical treatment when they need it. Some hospitals, in fact, will not even admit emergency patients who cannot prove they can pay their bill!

People need to become more aware of health problems, so they must be given more health education. In that way everyone learns to eat good food and to prevent disease.

Governments could also improve world health by protecting our environment. Tougher laws are needed to stop industry from polluting the air, soil and water. It is thought that 80 percent of cancers are caused by pollution. Every year half a million people are poisoned by pesticides.

What can governments in the South do?

Apart from these general considerations, governments in the South could improve health by spending more money on the rural areas where most people live. At present, resources are channeled into the cities, where the wealthy live, and the rural majority are neglected. Young people flock to the cities to seek work, and the cities become overcrowded. Several cities in the South now contain more than 20 million people, most of whom live in terrible slums.

Agricultural workers in the South often have to spray dangerous chemicals without the benefit of protective clothing.

A literacy class for women in India. At the moment, most development projects are aimed at men, but this is gradually beginning to change.

Women in the South must be educated so they can learn about good nutrition, immunization, hygiene, family planning and agriculture. The cheapest way to reduce infant mortality is to educate women. Women carry out most of the food production and processing in the South – yet they receive none of the training and technology for improving agriculture. The education of mothers is far more important than that of doctors, who see children only when they are ill. Mothers look after children every day, and keep them healthy. But educating doctors is more prestigious for governments than educating mothers. Unfortunately, few governments realize the importance of investing in women. Perhaps this is because most governments are dominated by men, and it is they who make the decisions.

Train a man and you train an individual; train a woman and you build a nation.
Bishop Nzimbe, Kenya, May 1985

Governments in the South could also spend more money on preventive health care and less on curative care and large hospitals. Hospitals are popular with doctors, politicians and the few patients who visit them, but they have little effect on the health of the majority of people. The planning of health services in the South has been patterned after those in the North, and not on the needs of the South.

> We must not be tempted by offers of big new hospitals with all the costs involved until at least every one of our citizens has a basic medical service readily available to him.
>
> *President Nyerere of Tanzania*

In 1985 several presidents launched campaigns to immunize every child in their country. President Evren of Turkey himself immunized the first child in a campaign to reach 5 million children and save 500 lives every week. Prime Minister Rajiv Ghandi has announced that every child in India should be immunized by 1990, as a living memorial to his mother, Indira Ghandi.

Of far more widespread use than specialist hospitals are trained community health workers. The poorer countries need many more of these workers, and governments must train them.

Improving health care in the South is a complex task, and many people need to work together to achieve it. Teachers, health workers and agricultural advisers must all work together for the good of their communities.

A training session for community health workers – the most cost-effective way of delivering health care.

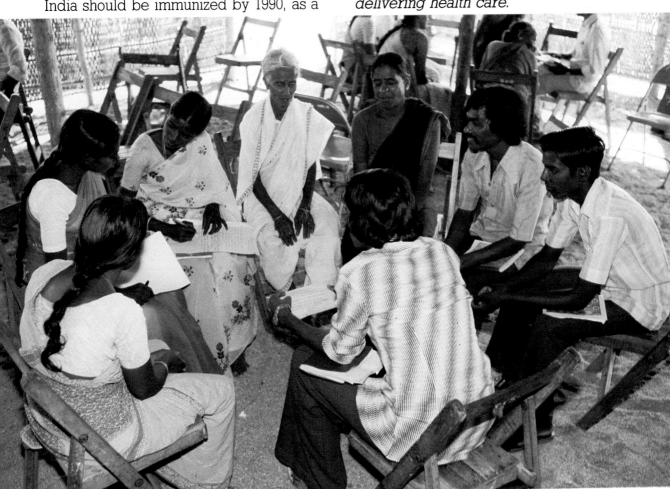

What can governments in the North do to help?

The best way for the North to help improve health care in the South is to assist its economic development. The countries of the North have great technical expertise, which they can share with the South. They also have vast resources of money, some of which is used for foreign aid. Much aid, however, is not given as money but as surplus goods manufactured in the donor country, such as cars or televisions. The president of Rwanda, in Africa, refused a gift of a television transmitting station from France. He said that his country could not afford to make its own programs, and the people could not afford to buy television sets. Radios would have been more appropriate. Many donor countries give money only to those governments that share their political beliefs.

Rich countries have become used to enjoying cheap imported goods, but so often these goods are cheap only because

A day's wages for this tea picker in Sri Lanka would hardly be enough to buy a cup of tea in the North.

the people who produce them have been paid desperately low wages. For example, a tea picker in Bangladesh is paid less than 75 cents *a day*, because we expect cheap tea. The richer countries must be prepared to pay more realistic prices for goods from the South.

We live in a divided world, in which some people are far more likely to enjoy good health than others. This is unjust. It is also dangerous, for the health, peace and economic development of the world depend on each other. If we are to improve this situation, governments and individuals alike must work together for freedom and equality. Priority must be given to improving the health of everyone in the world. Cutting the money spent on armaments and diverting this cash to health care would go a long way toward reducing sickness and suffering.

Glossary

Antibiotics Medicines that fight infections.

Antibodies Very small particles in the blood that fight diseases.

Birth spacing Having a space of at least three years between each child in the family

Calories The amount of energy that food contains.

Cassava A root crop grown in equatorial areas. Also called manioc.

Contraceptive Any method of preventing pregnancy.

Dehydration The loss of too much water from the body. It can be caused by diarrhea, bleeding, sweating, vomiting or severe burns. See Oral Rehydration Drink.

Diarrhea Runny or liquid feces.

Diphtheria A dangerous infectious disease of the throat, which kills or disables many children in the South.

Epidemiology The study of patterns of disease in a society. Epidemiologists look for possible causes of diseases.

Family planning Parents planning ahead how many children they will have.

Gross National Product The total value of the goods and services produced in a country in one year.

Immunization Injections or medicines given to prevent certain diseases.

Infant mortality rate The number of babies less than a year old that die compared to the number that are born.

Latrine A toilet dug in the earth.

Life expectancy The average number of years lived by people in a country.

Malaria A disease spread by mosquitoes. It causes a high fever, anemia, and bad headaches and can be fatal. It can be prevented by medicines and the control of mosquitoes.

Malnourishment Lack of adequate nutrition, or a bad diet. Overweight people are malnourished if they eat too many sweets and fats.

Measles A disease affecting the skin, lungs and eyes. It can be prevented by immunization. Undernourished children may die or go blind from measles.

North and **South** The same as "industrialized" and "less developed" countries.

Nutrition The eating and digestion of food and its effect on the body.

Oral Rehydration Drink A mixture of water, sugar and salt taken by mouth to prevent and treat dehydration.

Pesticides Poisonous chemicals sprayed onto crops to kill insects and plant diseases.

Pharmaceutical company A company that makes and sells medicines and drugs.

Pneumonia An infection of the lungs, causing fever, pain, and sometimes death if not treated.

Polio A disease that can cause paralysis. It is common in the South, but now rare in the North. It can be prevented by immunization.

Politicians The people in government who make the laws and take the decisions about how resources will be used.

Primary health care Preventing disease through good sanitation, nutrition, immunization and education.

Resources The land and all that can be extracted from it and grown on it. A country's resources includes its people, their skills, and their commitment to their society.

Sanitation Public hygiene measures, including clean water supplies, sewage and waste disposal systems.

Smallpox An infectious disease of the skin that was once common everywhere. Now it no longer exists.

Staple foods The foods most commonly eaten in a society. Wheat, used to make bread, is a staple food in the United States. Zambia's staple food is corn.

Tetanus A serious disease that kills adults and children if they have not been immunized. It enters the body through cuts and wounds. Tetanus kills many newborn babies in the South if their umbilical cords are not kept clean and their mothers are not immunized.

Third World A name used to describe the less developed countries. Most Third World countries are in the southern hemisphere and many were once colonies of Western countries.

Tuberculosis (TB) A serious disease that usually affects the lungs. It can be prevented by immunization and good nutrition.

Undernourishment Not eating enough food.

UNICEF United Nations Children Fund, which works all over the world helping children.

Vaccine The medicine used in immunization.

Whooping cough A dangerous disease that can kill babies or damage their lungs. It can be prevented by immunization.

Picture Acknowledgments

The publisher would like to thank the following for permission to reproduce the pictures in this book: Camera Talks 16; Mary Evans Picture Library 11; Format Photographers (Jenny Matthews) 25 (top), 27, 41; Janie Hampton 15, 23; John and Penny Hubley cover, 12, 13, 17, 21, 25 (bottom), 30, 34, 37, 38, 39, 40; Hutchison frontispiece (W. Jesco v. Puttkamer), 26; Save the Children Fund (Penny Tweedie) 9, 14, 19, 20, (Jenny Matthews) 29; Topham 22, 24, 35; ZEFA 36; all artwork is by Malcolm Walker.

Books to read

AIDS by Alan E. Nourse, M.D. (Watts, 1986)

Know about AIDS by Margaret O. Hyde and Elizabeth H. Forsyth, M.D. (Walker, 1987)

Understanding AIDS by Ethan A. Lerner, M.D., Ph.D. (Lerner, 1987)

Hunger and Malnutrition in America by Gerald Leinwand (Watts, 1985)

The Third World Today by Richard Worth (Watts, 1983)

Further information

American Association for World Health
2001 "S" St., N.W., Suite 530
Washington, D.C. 20009

This is the U.S. organization affiliated with the World Health Organization headquartered in Geneva, Switzerland.

Oxfam America
115 Broadway
Boston, MA 02116

Oxfam (from Oxford Committee for Famine Relief) is a worldwide network begun in England in 1942. The disaster assistance organization funds self-help projects in poor countries and responds to emergency needs.

Save the Children Federation
54 Wilton Road
Westport, CT 06880

This voluntary agency assists children, families, and communities in the U.S. and abroad to advance social and economic stability through community development and family self-help projects.

La Leche League International
9616 Minneapolis
Franklin Park, IL 60131

The goal of this organization is to ban advertising and promotion of breast-milk substitutes, particularly in Third World countries.

UNICEF
United Nations
New York, NY 10017

Dedicated to addressing problems and needs of children in both industrialized and developing countries, UNICEF works with goverments worldwide to develop and implement social service, health, nutrition, and educational programs.

Index